D0049462

_____

_____

i am THE CAT

 KPT PUBLISHING

i am THE CAT

Copyright © 2017 by KPT Publishing
Written by Liz Abeler Blaylock

Published by KPT Publishing
Minneapolis, Minnesota 55406
www.KPTPublishing.com

ISBN 978-1-944833-02-2

Design by David Abeler
Production by Koechel Peterson and Associates, Minneapolis, Minnesota

First printing March 2017

10 9 8 7 6 5 4 3 2

Printed in the United States of America

Can't look away,

can you.

I am so beautiful
that you shouldn't

look at me.

Don't look away!

I know it's 3 a.m.,

but tell me again
that I'm a pretty cat.

I can't eat this food.
It's *too* fresh...

now it's too stale.

Take it away!

Nap or litterbox?

Well, why don't you use
your treadmill?

Remember all those *fun* rides in the car?

Me neither.

Can you pet me?
What do you mean,
   I'm out of reach?

Your love grows cold.

I'm glad you're home.
  I hate it
    when you're gone.

I want to be alone now.

Oh well,
what would I do
if I caught it?

There's cat hair on
your sweater.
Oh, *it's mine*?

Maybe
we should see
other people.

I'm sorry for that
bad thing I did.

How did
you know that
African violets
are my *favorite* salad?

What do you mean
"I'm hatching
a plot?"

I'm spontaneous.

That purring noise
I make when I'm content?
the vet said it could also
be from anxiety…

*or from
plotting mischief.*

Yes, I knocked over
your plant,
the one *you* forget to water.

My way of killing it
was faster,
more *merciful.*

I shred your couch.
You spill coffee on it.
Potay-to, potah-to.

You think
I said "Meow?"

I said *"Now!"*

What?
You taunt and tempt
me with string?

No! Don't take it away.

What do you mean,
you couldn't find me.
I was in one of my
27 favorite
hiding places,

watching you
look for me.

Sometimes
I forget
I used to be
a *wild* animal.

There's a bug
on the floor
in the corner.

You might want
to get rid of it…

before I eat half of it
and cough up the rest.

You say
"Behavior is
communication."

Well, if you're
so smart,
look in your shoe
and tell me
what I said.

TV is so annoying.
Turn it off and pet me.

No, wait—
let's watch this
annoying cat food
commercial first.

I feel like I need to
make friends,
be loyal,
show affection
and generally be nice.

I'll be napping
until the feeling
goes away.

Sometimes
I forget
I'm *not*
a wild animal.

I'll keep looking...

until next time.

ABOUT THE AUTHOR

LIZ ABELER BLAYLOCK lives in messy house in Minnesota with her husband, daughter, grandson, parents (downstairs in the "mother-in-law" apartment—and yes, their part of the house is not messy,) two goldfish, and a beautiful cat named Lucy.

By day, Liz works with middle school students with special needs. By night, Liz makes dinner, does laundry, moving piles of stuff from one place to another, and makes time for her cat.

> *"I marvel at the intricate, beautiful and fearful working of creation, and revel in the grace and mercy of the Creator."*

Hope you enjoyed my memories!